TO

FROM

DATE

New York Times Best-Selling Author

JEN HATMAKER

7 DAYS OF

CHRISTMAS

A Season of Generosity

7 DAYS OF CHRISTMAS

A SEASON OF GENEROSITY

Copyright © 2019 by Hatmaker Partners, LLC

Published in association with Yates & Yates, www.yates2.com.

Library of Congress Cataloging-in-Publication Data has been requested.

ISBN 978-1-5018-8827-4

Scripture quotations are taken from the Common English Bible, copyright 2011. Used by permission.
All rights reserved.
Interior Design by Dexterity, in collaboration with Linda Bourdeaux
Cover Design by Micah Kandros

19 20 21 22 23 24 25 26—10 9 8 7 6 5 4 3 2 1
MANUFACTURED IN THE PEOPLE'S REPUBLIC OF CHINA

To Jesus.

Long lay the world in sin and error pining, until you appeared and the soul felt its worth.

"Nearby shepherds were living in the fields,
guarding their sheep at night.
The Lord's angel stood before them, the Lord's
glory shone around them,
and they were terrified.
The angel said, "Don't be afraid! Look! I
bring good news to you—wonderful,
joyous news for all people.
Your savior is born today in David's city.
He is Christ the Lord."

—LUKE 2:8-11

CONTENTS

A New Season

People want to talk to me about tons of things when they meet me in public. I field plenty of questions about really, really important stuff like homemade pizza dough, surviving middle school programs, chicken maintenance, and Gilmore Girls. I am obviously here to serve the world with my special knowledge, so I am always happy to oblige.

But if I had to choose the one venture folks still want to hash out with me, it is all things related to my book *7: An Experimental Mutiny Against Excess*. The little project that could maintain life and energy year after year. People are fascinated. They kind of want to try it. They did try it and want to tell me about wearing the same pair of leggings for a month. They are curious about what stuck in our family, what we still practice.

If it seems I am talking in code, here is the short-hand version of 7: plagued by my own sense of unchecked excess, lazy consumerism, and careless waste, I invited (read: forced) my family into a seven-month experiment to tackle seven areas where we were spinning out of control: food, clothes, spending, waste, media and technology, possessions, and stress. All seven areas marked by too much, too selfish, too consumed, or too unhealthy. How much did we spend a month? I had no idea. How many hours were we wasting on screens? Not sure, but it felt like a lot.

So in the spirit of a fast, a temporary restraint on our appetites for spiritual connection, we dialed down our choices in each area to just seven, one month at a time: only seven foods for a month, we wore the same seven pieces of clothes for a month, spent money in only seven places, adopted seven green practices, eliminated seven forms of media and technology, gave away seven things we owned a day, and practiced the "seven sacred pauses"—seven scheduled daily moments of specific prayer and meditation.

Spoiler alert: it changed our lives.

We didn't really know how it would all go, of course. It seemed bananas or, as my friend said, *eccentric*. Turns out we were an unregulated mess in every area, so taming the chaos while committing to learn, study, press, evaluate . . . it was like drinking from a fire hose. There was a great deal we didn't know about conservation and labor supply chains, local economics and stress-induced anxiety, technology brain patterns, and sustainable farming. Do you see what I'm saying? Scratch the surface and you end up down the rabbit hole of best practices in the textile industry. I pulled up my chair to the table of dozens, maybe hundreds of experts, practitioners, spiritual leaders, and global experts and finally got my head around my place in creation, in community, and in culture.

Interestingly, the actual 7 experiment, taking into account seven months of real time practice plus a few

weeks in between for processing and writing started in January and ended on Thanksgiving. Exactly one month was left out of its gaze: December. For a project focused on consumerism and excess, *December now seems like a very strange season to leave out.* I didn't do this on purpose, but I never applied the principles of 7 to the month in which Americans spent $721 billion dollars last year. The month in which we get swept up, caught up, and jacked up. The month in which one of my children who shall remain unnamed described his Christmas disappointment like this: "Why can't I just get a horse?"

So with great anticipation, I put this delicious book in your hands as we all steer our ships into a season spiritually marked by great tenderness but economically marked by great excess. It is the strangest dichotomy. We all feel it. I do. You do. We have a strong sense that the tail is wagging the dog, but with near constant propaganda from every conceivable angle, it is a sincere challenge to jump off the crazy train and reclaim one of our holiest seasons.

But if the results of the rest of 7 are any indicator, we actually have great control over how we celebrate Christmas and thus how it affects our families, communities, and hearts. We are not helpless victims of Black Friday. We are not stuck spending more than we have. We don't have to hand over our Christmas joy to culture. We can reclaim its beauty, reinvent its rhythms, restore its delight. We are in charge of our own lives! It is more than possible to experience a Christmas season focused on connectivity and love and generosity and Jesus, the greatest joy to the world.

Some of this book pulls from the original 7 content, so those of you who read the book will recognize a few parts, but the main content is finally filling in what the source material left out: Christmas. What a delight to take the lessons of 7 and apply them to this season!

There is so much goodness here. My hope is that you are able to join hands with the dearest people in your life and celebrate in freedom. We have permission to leave the most exhausting, draining parts of Christmas behind and grab onto all its joy, all its wonder, all its magic. Jesus is enough, as it turns out.

One last note before you dive in: I have given you tons of ideas, activities, and suggestions for a meaningful Christmas, and the worst thing in the world would be interpreting them as a checklist. On the contrary! These are only options; pick what works for your family. Pick the easiest one. Pick the funnest one. Pick your favorite one. Pick the one that works. Pick the one you like. Pick the one that gives you back some sanity. No Christmas shame here! Never! These are meant to restore the season, not add to its pressure. Steer your own ship! This month is yours to make beautiful.

So welcome to *7 Christmas*! May it set you free to celebrate in a manner worthy of a King who came to us not on a throne but in a manger. Who chose shepherds as His witnesses and the sky as His choir loft. Who came in the simplest forms to the simplest people and still managed to save the world. Jesus, Lord at thy birth.

ONE

Kitchen

*"It is written: 'Man shall not
live on bread alone,
but on every word that comes
from the mouth of God.'"*

—MATTHEW 4:4

1

After the Casseroles

If you're anything like me, the Christmas holiday season heightens all my senses. I love the excitement of it all—family and friends coming together, people being just a little nicer than normal, a deepened sense of communion with God, and, of course, playing in the snow.

Well, it happened that one time in Austin. We had a few snowflakes and the city went hysterical like it was a sign of the apocalypse. Meanwhile, all five kids were running around the front yard in shorts— *shorts*, Austin's winter dress code—and trying to catch enough flakes to roll a teeny tiny snowball worth hurling at the nearest sibling.

In reflecting on the millions of reasons to be joyous, one of my favorites is food. I'm sure that's the greatest shock of your life.

If you've followed the adventures of my family through the writing and surviving of 7 (just kidding), you know that one of the most difficult—but also one of the most rewarding pieces of that journey revolves around food. Where we get it from. How often we eat—if we eat at all. What choices we make. How we can share and give back and be more aware of those around us. And how we can be hungry and full at the same time.

We're fast upon the time of year when many families across the country will be eating Thanksgiving leftovers and cursing their scales in the wake of overindulgence (I'm looking at you, chocolate pie), the shine will have worn off of our hoarded Black Friday purchases. This year, instead of watching everyone sit around the living room shopping on their phones, giving thanks by ignoring each other politely in the quest for $50 off the sixteenth television for their homes, what if we started a new tradition?

From my own experiences, I can testify that a simpler meal—and the joy surrounding it all—inspired gratitude in my family, even though it wasn't on Thanksgiving. And that pure spirit of giving can be found anywhere, if you look for it.

My challenge to you—if you're up for some out-of-the-box fun (Oh, come on! It'll be great!), use some imagination, a dash of creativity, and a handful of good cheer as we dive into some of my favorites! In this next section, I'll be listing some ways you and yours can take intentional steps this Christmas season to embrace the 7 experience by rejecting excess, and in doing so, capture the spirit of generosity at the heart of the holiday season. I promise you'll find yourself helped too, right in the middle of it all.

As always, these are suggestions (patting myself on the back) to get you started, but I know you can think of a dozen other ideas that resonate with your heart and tribe, and can make a big impact right where you live and work and play. The point is not to check off what's on *my list*, so much as to be all in on whatever God's put in front of *you*. Even the seemingly smallest gesture can make a big impact when delivered with love and care.

Favorites

If there's one word I want you to remember this week besides Jesus (Oh, and dessert, so that makes two), it's *intentionality*. The days correlated with the 7 experiment won't impact our holiday spirits in the same way if we just give from the discard pile. Oops. And yes, I know I've done this before so don't think I'm judging you. Sidebar: Do you know how long a can of baked beans can hide out in the back of your pantry? *Decades.*

All that to say, donating that six-year-old can of Van Camp's Pork and Beans that your mother-in-law bought but didn't eat while staying at your house that time— that there is zero chance of your family ever consuming anyway—it's just not going to feel the same to your sweet, giving heart. You wouldn't eat those crusty beans, right? So why would you expect someone else to?

Here are some kitchen-related favorites for 7-styled food experiences:

- WHEN YOU DO DONATE FOOD ITEMS, instead of hauling them out of the dark recesses of your kitchen, bring them right from the grocery store. Make it a fun family affair and get everyone involved. Imagine you're shopping for a family just like yours, and have everyone in your family pick out their favorite seven food items to give to someone in need.

- READY FOR A BIGGER CHALLENGE? In a counterbalance to our American Thanksgiving feasting, take a day to eat seven simple foods (organic and locally sourced, if possible) and reflect on the significant segment of the world's beautiful humans who don't have 240 items in their pantries like I did. If you're reading this before Thanksgiving, consider reducing the

Thanksgiving meal to seven foods. Even if it means the cranberry sauce doesn't make the cut.

- TALK WITH THE FAMILY TRIBE ABOUT FAVORITE HOLIDAY FOODS, and select a number of them to make and give to someone else, but not necessarily to have for yourselves. This could be a starter, a casserole, a dessert, or a family favorite. Again, if you happen to be reading this before Thanksgiving, give those dishes to a friend, neighbor, or stranger. (If you're giving food to a total stranger, you'd better introduce yourself and your purpose first so they don't think you're trying to drug them with Aunt Maybelle's Famous Squash Casserole.)

- GO HELP OUT AT A SOUP KITCHEN the weekend after Thanksgiving weekend or during Christmas week, when most of the volunteers have come and gone. What about after the holidays, too? If you think your kitchen cabinets need reorganizing, sweet baby Jesus, you can bet those food pantries need help every day of the week. If your organizational skills would make Marie Kondo proud, spark some joy by giving your time, whether it's seven hours or seven days, to a kitchen that serves others.

JEN'S
HOLIDAY
DIAL·IT·DOWN

FROM THE SOCIALS

Annual PSA: No one is interested in my deconstructed green bean casserole with bourbon cream sauce and pickled shallots. They want canned green beans mixed with cream of mushroom soup topped with shelf-stable fried onions. I cannot be precious about reinventing American Thanksgiving staples for these jokers.

I

CANNOT

BE

Precious

ABOUT

REINVENTING

American

Staples

FOR THESE

JOKERS.

Reflections on Generosity

Thinking back to my month of food deprivation, um, I mean limitations, in 7, midway through the month we had a holiday celebration centered on gratitude and rest. The kind of simple generosity that I so want to be at the heart of my holiday. Cue flashback scene, *now*.

I had a glorious, marvelous 7 evening.

It started with a dinner invite, although this would typically be disastrous. (When consulting The Council—my group of six friends, advisors, and the personal think tank that kept the wheels on the original 7 experiment—on what to do when people cook for me or take me to dinner, they advised, "Don't be an imbecile.") I tell people the basics of 7 and hope for the best when I'm not in control of the kitchen.

Anyhow, this dinner invite was safe because it

was Council Member Susana's parents, Dale and Laurel, who'd already navigated Pick Five with her. Laurel asked about my seven foods in advance, so I didn't waste any emotional space worrying about an impending evasion.

Dale and Laurel are Messianic Jews who go to our church along with most of their giant family/commune. We arrived at 6:00, just as the sun was setting. The table boasted a beautiful presentation of all seven foods. It was so dear and thoughtful, I almost burst into tears.

Traditionally, on Friday afternoon, observant Jews begin Shabbat, or Sabbath, preparations. The mood is like preparing for the arrival of a special, beloved guest: the house is cleaned, the family dresses up, the best dishes are set, and a festive meal is prepared—in our case, a 7-inspired meal. Shabbat candles are lit and a blessing recited just before sunset. This ritual, performed by the woman of the house, officially marks the beginning of Shabbat.

The two candles represent two commandments: *zakhor* ("remember" creation and God's deliverance from captivity) and *shamor* ("observe" the day of rest God initiated at creation). Dale led us through a traditional Kiddush, a prayer over wine sanctifying Shabbat while passing a loaf of challah, a sweet bread shaped into a braid.

We shared some beautiful readings of Scripture together (until the Hebrew parts when Brandon and I stayed silent to not butcher this lovely moment with atrocious pronunciation). Dale and Laurel sang a few sections, and the whole thing was beautiful. Between the communion, the food prepared with loving hands, the Scripture, and the ancient rhythm of it all, I was overjoyed.

There are many Shabbat readings available, but this one I love:

There are days when we seek
things for ourselves

and measure failure by what we do not gain.

On the Sabbath we seek not to acquire
but to share.

There are days when we exploit nature

as if it were a horn of plenty
that can never be exhausted.

On the Sabbath we stand in wonder before
the mystery of creation.

There are days when we act as if
we cared nothing

for the rights of others.

On the Sabbath we are reminded that justice is our
duty and a better world our goal.

Therefore we welcome Shabbat.

Day of rest, day of wonder, day of peace.

Final Thoughts

"Yet even now, says the LORD, return to me with all your hearts, with fasting, with weeping, and with sorrow; tear your hearts and not your clothing. Return to the LORD your God, for he is merciful and compassionate, very patient, full of faithful love, and ready to forgive."

—JOEL 2:12-13

When I wrote about all of this at the end of my first month of the 7 experiment, I made some interesting conclusions. Initially, the ordering of the seven months was fairly random; food received slot one because I copied this concept from Susana, and that's what she did. Rest got the seventh slot because God rested on the seventh day, and that seemed poetic. Other than that, the months were listed in brainstorm order.

That said, I'm grateful food launched me out of the starting blocks. There was no shirking possible, no viable semi-attention. Seven foods required my concentration from morning until night every day. Each meal was intentional, each bite calculated. There was no escape from 7; I never had longer than five hours between meals to mentally slip away. The concept of reduction was never further than my next meal.

This held me fast to the heart of Jesus.

In *Simplicity*, Richard Rohr wrote,

> On the way to contemplation we do the same thing that
> Jesus Christ did in the wilderness. Jesus teaches us not
> to say, "Lord, Lord," but to do the will of His Father.
> What must primarily concern us is that we do what
> Jesus has bidden us do. Jesus went into the wilderness,
> ate nothing for forty days, and made himself empty.
> Of course, emptiness in and of itself isn't enough. The
> point of emptiness is to get ourselves out of the way so
> that Christ can fill us up. As soon as we're empty, there's
> a place for Christ, because only then are we in any
> sense ready to recognize and accept Christ as the totally
> other, who is not me.[1]

Honestly, I've said a lot of "Lord, Lord" without
simply doing the will of my Father. My mission is
clouded by a thousand elements with no eternal value.

The canvas is muddy. I know the correct Christian rhetoric—emptiness, surrender, humility—but those words are meaningless until they are more than words. While my life is marked by ambition, accumulation, and perceived success, then no matter how much I squawk about Jesus, I'm a resounding gong, a clanging symbol; I am nothing.

After Jesus' fast, He began healing, rescuing, redeeming. The Spirit filled up the emptiness Jesus created, launching Him into ministry. In some supernatural way the abstinence from food was the catalyst for Jesus' unveiling; the real fireworks were next. Never again would Jesus fly under the radar. His powerful ministry was activated, inviting worship and opposition, salvation and death. After thirty years on earth, His story truly began.

*"He ate nothing during those days
and afterward Jesus was starving."*

—LUKE 4:2

I AM HUNGRY.

THERE'S A BIG WORLD OUT

THERE THAT'S HUNGRY.

May my kitchen

FILL THAT HUNGER THIS

HOLIDAY SEASON.

TWO

Fashion

"While they were there, the time came
for Mary to have her baby.
She gave birth to her firstborn child,
a son, wrapped him snugly,
and laid him in a manger,
because there was no place for them
in the guestroom."

—LUKE 2:6-7

2

Aware of What We Wear

Whether you're into glittery red Christmas heels or sweaters with jingle bells sewn on them, there's often a pressure to *present well* during the holidays (and pretty much always), that our identity as women and wives and moms somehow hinges on how sparkly and spectacular our Christmas everything is, including our wardrobe.

How often have you dashed off to buy a new Christmas outfit for a holiday gathering? It's cute, I'm sure. But the more holiday specific it is, the fewer times you'll actually wear it again. Plus, did you really *need* it in the first place? What's wrong with the closet full of clothing you already have?

And we can't forget about those ugly Christmas sweater parties. That's one terrible outfit you'll only wear once, even though you put soooo much effort into the hunt.

I know, I know. Retail therapy is fun for some, and I'm not taking that away from you. But perhaps this is one area that might benefit from some 7 restraint! If we can be more aware of the outside expectations during the holiday season, maybe we can do more with what we already have, so we can find fun ways to help others who have less. And I should know about the more bit, because I had way more than I thought I did.

If you read 7, you judged me (and rightly so) when I

confessed that there were 327 items of clothing in my closet, not including socks, undies, bras, and the like.

Don't lie, I know you did.

You were shocked. Aghast! *How can someone so pious and thoughtful own so many articles of clothing? How can she say she loves Jesus when she owns twenty-three pairs of shoes?* You thought. And then, curiosity piqued, you walked into your bedroom, looked into your closet, opened your dresser drawers, and did a quick visual count of the items. My guess is you winced within the first forty five-seconds and likely stopped all together once you hit triple digits and realized you weren't even halfway through your drawer of tee shirts. I'm speaking for a friend.

But it's okay. The first step in admitting you have a fashion crisis on your hands is admitting you have more than you need to begin with. Truth is, many of us do.

So, no, I'm not going to make you choose only seven

items to wear for the next month, especially during the Christmas season, so quit stressing. But I am suggesting that you make the time to do a self-audit on just how much you do own, so you know what you're working with.

Yes, depending on where you live, there are seasons. We have them, too, in Austin. Kind of. Yes, I know fashion changes. I am aware that you might need a blend of business wear and casual wear and active wear and sleep wear and whatever else.

But do we really need forty shirts? Really? Five still have tags on them. Two of them we didn't like to begin with but bought them anyway because they were on sale. At least one fits poorly. And there are always those few items that we can't bear to part with, because we've had them since college, or high school, or birth, or the Renaissance, and . . . I get it. But in the end, surely we have excess items to donate, right?

This season, try to be more aware of what you purchase, and why, and when. And once you've gone through your own items, you can lead the charge for the rest of your household.

Favorites

I'm not expecting you to Marie Kondo your closet, especially now during Christmas, when you're probably just trying to stay sane. But…if you have the time and inclination to tackle a little at a time, I promise it will be worth it. Because I've done this exercise before, I know how initially terrifying but fun (in the end) it can be.

If you are the type to go all-in on a challenge, this suggestion is for you. The first step is to clear everything out of your closet and dressers and separate them by categories. Tally up the numbers and write them down. Go ahead, it's great for shock value!

Socks:

Shoes:

Undies/bras:

Shirts:

Pants:

Dresses:

Accessories:

Jewelry:

And anything else that counts as wearable fashion (yes, tights and leggings should be counted. And flip-flops count as well. *All of them*. These items do not get to remain neutral like the Switzerland of clothing).

If just the thought of doing a half-day closet makeover gives you hives, here's an easier suggestion. Look through what you have and see if you can find seven items you no longer wear (or have never worn), to donate. That's it. If you're still feeling a little more adventurous, cull another seven items, and repeat until you feel both a sense of accomplishment and a knowing sense of peace that *these items* might be exactly what someone else truly needs.

Once you've worked through your stash, it's the perfect time for a come-to-Jesus moment as you stand there, looking at your glorious pile of fabrics and prints, solids and various textures, good decisions and questionable ones, different seasons and sizes—all in a jumbled heap before you, taking up space. And time. And money.

Now, answer these questions: How many feet do you have? (Answer zero-two . . . perhaps three if you live near any radioactive sites. And if so, sorry. And maybe you should move.)

How many torsos, legs, necks, wrists, and heads do you have?

My point is that you only have one body to clothe— regardless of appendages and preferences. So how many items of clothes do you actually *need*? Fewer than you own, I'm guessing. Great! Guess who could use those extra items? Other people! Especially during the Christmas season when temperatures are lower everywhere but Florida and Texas.

In true Christmas spirit, here are some 7-styled ideas for what to do with your family's extra items of clothing.

- FIRST THINGS FIRST: if it's dirty, torn, or otherwise unusable, please don't donate it. Instead, consider throwing it away or recycling, if possible. And for the love of Pete, do not donate used underwear. I know *you* know better, clearly, because you're a decent human. But *someone* keeps donating underwear to thrift stores because every time I walk into a Goodwill, there's a small section of single tighty-whities on pants hangers, just hanging there, exposed to the world. Same goes for used socks. Just trash them or keep a few to use as cleaning mitts around the house. (They're great for cleaning windows and mirrors!)

- FIND A FRIEND who wears the same shoe size you do, and give her one pair of shoes that you know you've only worn once or twice.

- AS A FAMILY, pick seven of your favorite items of clothing, those signature items, and give them to a friend as a sentimental gift. If you have a teen who is constantly borrowing your favorite comfy sweatshirt, wrap it up for her. She's going to continue to steal it anyway.

- IF YOU HAVE TO BE OUT SHOPPING ON BLACK FRIDAY, pick a family in need, whether from your church or workplace or charitable organization of choice, and intentionally find clothing for that family instead of purchasing for yourself that weekend.

- INSTEAD OF GOING FOR HIGH FASHION, GO FOR SYMBOLISM. Give away seven pairs of gloves as a family with a note pledging to help them—gardening gloves with a promise to help with spring work, work gloves with a pledge to help a friend with a project. Your kids might get involved, giving a pair of kitchen gloves with a promise to help with the dishes over the holidays. (Well, we can dream, right?)

- CALL THE COUNSELOR from an under-resourced school in your city and ask if she has a student or family that could use some clothes and shoes. Find a need, meet a need.

JEN'S
HOLIDAY
DIAL·IT·DOWN

FROM THE SOCIALS

Christmas 2017

Just keep plugging away. Sometimes things work like you wanted and sometimes they don't. Take your Christmas expectations into the month of December, sure, but hold them very, very loosely. Don't white knuckle everyone into manufactured joy and constant delight. Expect things to go exactly average or slightly under average, and if it happens to go north of that, well then Merry Christmas to all and to all a good night.

TAKE YOUR

Christmas

Expectations

FOR THE MONTH
OF DECEMBER,
BUT HOLD THEM

Very

Loosely.

Reflections on Generosity

When I first did the 7 experiment, on day twenty-five of Clothing month, I was able to reflect on our purchasing trends as a family and the many reasons (read: excuses) behind some of those purchases. Want to know the reason I had 327 items of clothes in my closet to begin with? Because I could. (Oh, and by the way, in case you didn't read 7, do that. And then, yes, be disgusted that I did, in fact, have 327 articles of clothing.) Maybe part of the reason was a bit of consumer brainwashing mixed with the desire to "fit in," but mostly it was greed.

Every time I buy another shirt I don't need or a seventh pair of shoes for my daughter, I redirect my powerful dollar to the pockets of consumerism, fueling my own greed and widening the gap. Why? Because I like it. Because those are cute. Because I want that.

These thoughts burden me holistically, but the trouble is, I can rationalize them individually. This one pair of shoes? Big deal. This little outfit? It was on sale. This micro-justification easily translates to nearly every purchase I've made. Alone, each item is reduced to an easy explanation, a harmless transaction. But all together, we've spent enough to irrevocably change the lives of a hundred thousand people. What did I get for that budgeting displacement? Closets full of clothes we barely wear and enough luxuries to outfit twenty families.

What if all my silly little individual purchases *do* matter? What if I joined a different movement, one that was less enticed by luxuries and more interested in justice? What if I believed every dollar spent is vital, a potential soldier in the war on inequality?

When thirty-five years of choices overwhelm me, Jesus makes it simple again: "Love your neighbor as yourself." If you read the story, you'll see that Jesus takes a broad, global, interracial view of who our neighbor is. In other words, what standard is acceptable for my own life? My own family? This is the benchmark for everyone else, which necessitates a decrease in the definition of *necessary* (for us) and an increase in the definition of *acceptable* (for everyone else).

The average human gets around twenty-five thousand days on this earth, and most of us in the United States of America will get a few more. That's it. This life is a breath. Heaven is coming fast, and we live in that thin space where faith and obedience have relevance. We have this one life to offer; there is no second chance, no Plan B for the good news. We get one shot at living to expand the kingdom, fighting for justice. We'll stand before Jesus once, and none of our luxuries will accompany us. We'll have one moment to say, "This is how I lived."

More than thirteen thousand of those days are over for me. I'm determined to make the rest count.

Final Thoughts

> "*The first question which the priest and the Levite asked was: 'If I stop to help this man, what will happen to me?' But the good Samaritan reversed the question: 'If I do not stop to help this man, what will happen to him?'*"
>
> **—MARTIN LUTHER KING JR.**

In the grand scheme of things, "how I look to people" all of a sudden just seems ludicrous. Sure, it's a good idea to be clothed so we don't get arrested for public indecency, but do people really care that much about what we look like and what we wear every day? And if they do, isn't that their problem and not ours?

In a culture that elevates beauty and style, the Christian community is at genuine risk for distraction, even deception. What do we truly admire in our leaders? Are we no different from the secular population, drawn to charisma and style above substance and integrity?

I hope not.

Just look at Jesus, who showed up in this world wearing swaddling clothes—basically an old blanket—and gave us a glimpse at what it means to be present without *presenting*. He was not wearing a designer onesie. Still, the wise men bowed down before Him.

The Jesus who told us about flowers of the field that don't stress out about matching shoes but are dressed by God like nobody's business, wants us *present*, not dressed up. He invites us in some small way this season to recognize that we have and are enough and, in doing so, be freed to give and clothe and breathe in His presence this season.

I want to belong to a Christian community known for a different kind of beauty, the kind that heals and inspires. We cannot carry the gospel to the poor and lowly while emulating the practices of the rich and powerful or worrying too much about how we look or what outfit we chose that day. We've been invited into a story that begins with humility and ends with glory; never the other way around.

Let's align ourselves correctly, sharing in the humble ministry of Jesus, knowing one day we'll feast at His table in splendor. And He won't give a rip what we're wearing.

WE'VE BEEN INVITED INTO A

STORY THAT BEGINS WITH

Humility

AND ENDS WITH

Glory;

NEVER

THE OTHER WAY AROUND.

THREE

Stuff

"They entered the house and saw the child with Mary his mother. Falling to their knees, they honored him. Then they opened their treasure chests and presented him with gifts of gold, frankincense, and myrrh."

—MATTHEW 2:11

3

The Red and Green Rubbermaid Takedown

Somewhere in your home, there is a plastic container of Christmas decorations. *Scratch that.* There's a small village of containers of Christmas decorations. Every year, somehow, we need three more strands of Christmas lights. Last year's two-foot-tall nutcracker soldier is looking long in the tooth, and we need the latest electric black light disco snow globe to make our holiday décor complete. And Christmas ornaments? Clark Griswold's tree would look weighed down and

saggy with the ornament bling we're hauling down
from our attic every year.

And even so, how many times are we out early on the
26th to hoard what's left over? Because S-A-L-E.

Meanwhile, in this holiday frenzy to get, gather,
and display more, we're missing days of time with our
kids and families and friends. Half the time, we're so
exhausted from "getting," that by the time Aunt Lucy's
Christmas party comes around, we'd frankly rather
stay home watching *Christmas with the Kranks* in
sweatpants. Bah humbug.

You might recall that in one month's time, my initial
goal was to remove 210 items from our home. That
was seven items a day for thirty days. What might
seem ambitious for some seemed like a piece of cake
to me, and as far as the clothes go—it was. But some
of the other items were much harder than I thought.
Like blankets. I have an unnatural attachment to

blankets. And books. And movies. Sue me. I need to be comfortably entertained!

My guess is that you have several categories of items you can sort through that don't cause some kind of whackadoo response when you think about getting rid of what you don't use. Especially when it comes to Christmas decorations. Maybe you have a ton of festive pillows. Or four complete sets of collectible Christmas dishes you never use. What about the bins of old holiday wreaths you haven't touched in three years? *Meh*, you think. *Sure, I can get rid of those things. But don't you dare ask me to donate my ukulele collection!*

Whatever floats your boat, sister. The point of this exercise isn't to cause pain anyway. It's to alleviate someone else's pain; to make you aware of what you do have, what you don't really need, and who could benefit from receiving the things you don't really need. That's it. Simple as pie. Who can you bless today with things

you don't

need or want?

   Aaaand, while you're going
through your physical stuff, you can
also take this amazing opportunity to deal
with the mental stuff that comes with it.
It's like a two-for-one! Seriously. I get it.
There are emotions and memories associated
with many of the items you have, especially
ones you've had for years, decades even. But are
they keeping you captive? In other words—do you
own these items or do they own you? And if they own
you, why?

Do you feel guilty for not wanting to keep Aunt Brenda's walnut dining room table with eight chairs? Even if she's been dead for fifteen years? Well, I'm not the boss of you, clearly, but I don't think you should feel guilted into holding onto any family heirlooms that you don't actually want.

I guarantee you that someone, somewhere has been looking for a beautifully sturdy table just like yours to have their first Christmas dinner as a family, and they would die if they found it at your local thrift store. Or, better yet, donate it to a charity that helps establish housing for immigrants or one that gathers furniture for those transitioning back into society from prison.

I'm certain that Aunt Brenda is far too busy playing pinochle in the Great Hereafter to even notice who has her dining room table and chairs.

Favorites

When you put a positive spin on sorting and donating, it really does start to stir excitement in the soul. You're helping someone else—potentially lots of people, actually—and you're helping yourself by clearing out space in your beloved home.

Now, this new clean space you have isn't an excuse to rush out and buy, buy, buy, and to come home and fill those spaces back up with cinnamon-scented candles. Nope, it's an invitation to actually have less! And to feel the benefits of having less because you have more room to breathe, more peace from a not-so-cluttered home, less guilt from packed-to-brim closets, and frankly, fewer things to dust and clean or maneuver around, amIright?

- EVEN BEFORE TALKING ABOUT THE OUTGOING ITEMS, FIRST CONSIDER an attempt to reduce the inflow. Tell yourself that it's okay to go a season without buying new decorations, that it's okay if you don't bring *every single storage container* of decorations down from the attic.

- ONCE YOU GET A BOX OF DECORATIONS DOWN, try picking out your favorite seven decorative items with your family. Put out just those seven items for a week of the holiday season, and then consider how much more you want to pull out of the bins.

- TAKE A FAVORITE DECORATION, one with sentimental value, and give it to a friend who needs encouragement this holiday season. Tell her (or him) that you're thankful for their friendship this holiday.

- THERE ARE SO MANY FOLKS OUT THERE STRUGGLING to have a holiday season at all, and your church or work communities likely know of those families. Take a look at your Christmas ornaments, and pull enough of them that, along with a modest box of new ornaments, they will decorate someone else's tree. Make arrangements to give a family a Christmas tree and offer to decorate it with them, explaining that you want them to have a combination of new ornaments and ornaments that you've enjoyed on your Christmas tree in years past.

- YOU CAN USE THIS OPPORTUNITY TO LOVINGLY DECLUTTER YOUR KITCHEN. You know the sixteen appliances on your kitchen counter, and seven more in the cabinet that never make it out? I bet someone would love—and use—one of those handy gadgets!

- LOOKING TO DOWNSIZE WHILE HELPING SOMEONE ELSE? Give away an item from each room in the house. Furniture counts! Don't replace it, instead let the room have that much more open space.

JEN'S
HOLIDAY
DIAL·IT·DOWN

FROM THE SOCIALS

Christmas 2018

The longer I live, the more distilled it all gets: what matters, what counts, what I love, where I want to be, and what I will be glad I invested in forty years from now. Every year, I need a little less: less hustle, less busyness, less "success," less Big and More, less stuff. And I also need a little more: more family, more besties, more porches, more dinners at home, more laughter, more of our little church, more gratitude.

EVERY YEAR,

I NEED A LITTLE LESS:

Less Hustle,

LESS BUSYNESS,

Less "Success,"

LESS BIG AND MORE,

LESS STUFF.

Reflections on Generosity

"Before the Festival of Passover, Jesus knew that his time had come to leave this world and go to the Father. Having loved his own who were in the world, he loved them fully."

—JOHN 13:1

One year, in the midst of my purge, we cancelled service and took church downtown to the corner of 7th and Neches, where our homeless community is concentrated in Austin. We grilled thirteen hundred burgers and ate together. Our band led worship; then a powerful moment of solidarity, we shared Communion. It was a beautiful mess of dancing, tears, singing, and sharing. It wasn't an *us* and *them* moment; it was just the church, remembering the Passover Lamb and celebrating our liberation together.

Now, if we get one repetitive request when serving our homeless friends, it's this: "Do you have a bag?" (Could also be: Can I have that bag? Can I take that trash bag? Do you have a bag I can put this bag in?) So this was the perfect moment to give away seven of my nine purses, which were nice and roomy, just like the ladies want.

When the gals had a perfect view for maximum impact, I hollered:

"Hey girls! Anyone want one of . . . these?"

Cranberry red leather

Green with gold buckles

Chocolate brown bohemian bag

Turquoise with short handles

Burnt orange across-the-shoulder

Shiny black backpack bag

And one little purse I debated on bringing. It was a tiny thing, hot pink crocodile by Gianni Bini, functionally useless but fashionably magnificent. Our street girls want the biggest bags possible, since they carry everything they own. A wheelbarrow would be a huge hit. So my little vanity purse was a wildcard, but at the last second with a conspiratorial nudge from the Spirit, I threw it in.

Not surprisingly, it was the last purse left. What self-respecting homeless woman picks a hot pink purse that would barely carry her bus pass? Glamour handbags are only for women who have eight others and a house in which to stash them. So I stood there with my one little purse, when it's rightful owner, the one for whom I daresay that purse was stitched together, made a beeline for me.

She had on her holiday finest, tights included, though it was ninety degrees. Flouncy dress with—

what else?—hot pink flowers. Hair done in sections with matching beads, pink floppy hat on standby. Leather dress shoes polished to a sheen. Dainty ribbon necklace and rings on four fingers.

She was six-years-old. Her name was NeNe.

Never has a purse better matched its owner. She slipped that hot pink number over her arm and never put it down, not even to eat. Her mom looked at me and no words were necessary; mothers speak a silent language. I took her picture and fussed over her beauty and breathed a thank you to Jesus for the nudge.

While this experience originally took place during Easter, this story is every bit as meaningful for the holiday season. Jesus—our greatest Christmas gift— is a redeemer, a restorer in every way. His day on the cross looked like a colossal failure, but it was His finest moment. He launched a kingdom where the least will be the greatest and the last will be first, where the poor will be comforted and the meek will inherit the earth. Jesus brought together the homeless with the privileged and said, "You're all poor, and you're all beautiful." The cross leveled the playing field, and no earthly distinction is valid anymore. It is the most epic miracle in history.

That is why we celebrate. May we never become so enamored by the substitutions of this world that we forget.

I serve a Savior who finds a way to get pink purses to homeless six-year-old girls. What can you do this season to be a vessel of blessings for others?

Final Thoughts

"When I was a child, I used to speak like a child, reason like a child, think like a child. But now that I have become a man, I've put an end to childish things. Now we see a reflection in a mirror; then we will see face-to-face. Now I know partially, but then I will know completely in the same way that I have been completely known."

—1 CORINTHIANS 13:11-12

A child says "me." An adult says "us." Maturity deciphers need from want, wisdom from foolishness. Growing up means curbing appetites, shifting from "me" to "we," understanding private choices have social consequences and public outcomes. Let's be consumers who silence the screaming voice that yells, "I WANT!" and instead listens to the quiet "we need," the marginalized voice of the worldwide community we belong to.

We top the global food chain through no fault or credit of our own. I've asked God a billion times why I have so much while others have so little. Why do my kids get full bellies? Why does water flow freely from my faucets? Why do we get to go the doctor when we're sick? There is no easy answer. The *why* definitely matters but so does the *what*. What do we do with our riches? What do we do with our privileges? What should we keep? What should we share? I better address this inequality since Jesus clearly identified the poor as His brothers and sisters and my neighbor.

What if we tried together? What if a bunch of Christians wrote a new story, becoming consumers the earth is groaning for? I suspect we'd find that elusive contentment, storing up treasures in heaven like Jesus told us to. I'm betting our stuff would lose its grip, and we'd discover riches contained in a simpler life, a communal responsibility. *Money* is the most frequent theme in Scripture; perhaps the secret to happiness is right under our noses. Maybe we don't recognize satisfaction, because it is disguised as radical generosity, a strange misnomer in a consumer culture.

Richard Rohr described American Christians in *Simplicity*:

> We're just about to become adults, to honestly let the Gospel speak to us, to listen to what Jesus says, in no

uncertain terms, about poverty and about leading a simple life in this world, a life that shows trust in God and not in our own power and weapons. God never promised us security in this world. God promised us only truth and freedom in our hearts. What does all this mean for us? It means that we're on the way.[1]

Let's prove that theory correct.

JESUS,

Our Greatest Gift

A REDEEMER, A RESTORER

IN EVERY WAY.

FOUR

Streaming

"The Word became flesh and made his home among us. We have seen his glory, glory like that of a father's only son, full of grace and truth."

—JOHN 1:14

4

Stream 'Til We Scream

I stream. You stream. We all stream our multiple devices and endless media sites until our brains turn into mush, and we have the attention span of gnats at a nudist colony picnic! Not nearly as fun as the ice cream song, but you get the point. Being plugged in all the time is making us tune out—from our jobs, our families, and our lives—at alarming rates.

But that's how the world is now, some say.

My kids are always on the computer at school and for homework.

My husband has to be able to answer calls and emails at all times.

I want to be able to post thirteen bazillion pictures of my pets each day, and you can't stop me.

We can't help that our children are turning into robots who still don't clean their rooms.

I need Amazon to finish my Christmas shopping!

But is that really true? (Okay, well admittedly, Amazon is becoming an all-too-necessary evil for holiday survival.)

It seems like it's easier to go with the flow and allow nonstop access to electronics and social media, than to turn the incessant flow off. And a total blackout during holiday season would feel like incarceration for kids and their parents, so that won't work. But what about creating a better balance this Christmas?

We've been conditioned to bring out laptops and iPads at Thanksgiving dinner, so we can figure out who's leaving Nana with the leftover turkey while we make a Wal-Mart run. Or place sixteen Black Friday orders for special online-only items, because, well, we can. And because we really need a ninth television set in the house for that price, right?

The consumption craze was built long ago, in pre-streaming era media. Have you ever been the one holiday shamed, because you forgot to get three Thanksgiving newspapers at the gas station on the way and were responsible for the lack of sales papers to rummage through? It's not pretty.

Now there's this whole other thing, though. An endless stream of Pinterest boards and Instagram photos, a barrage of "My Christmas is more perfect than your Christmas" sentiments leave us trying to recreate that fireplace mantel from that post we saw

and cussing
Michael's for
not having that
same dang foil
that's in the
photo.

Comparison
will rob us of any
and all joy if we let
it. That's the complete
opposite of what we should
be feeling during the holiday
season. So it's our job to take a
stand on how much streaming we consume
and whose voice we listen to most.

You are still the authority on at least your own life,
if not the lives of little ones you may or may not have to
feed each day. That means, you not only get to set some

rules, you get to be the voice of reason in an otherwise chaotic world. Okay, that might sound too Pollyanna, but you can at least cut down on screen time each day so your eyes don't fall out of your head, and your kids don't become zombies, maybe?

Before you put a pox on my house, I'm not telling you to move to a cabin in the woods with no internet (although that would be nice for a week or two) until spring. I am, however, advocating for responsible viewing and streaming this season, making sure we have our priorities right.

While it might feel harder at first to break up with 24/7 access to absolutely everything, I bet that once you've made some small changes, you'll begin to realize just how nice it feels to unplug, to be "unreachable" or "away," and to have time to do those old-fashioned things you used to enjoy like reading physical books, gardening, playing sports, going for a walk, opening

Christmas presents, baking holiday cookies, or having a nice and longer-than-ten-second conversation with those other humans you cohabitate with.

Favorites

When I tried this portion of the 7 challenge, it was really hard at first. I won't lie. It was hard enough for me to hold myself accountable, so enforcing the same rules on sometimes unruly children and a skeptical husband was not exactly easy. But by day twelve, I was really feeling good about it and my house felt peaceful. I even got to do things I hadn't done in weeks or months like:

- Cooking

- Taking walks after dinner with the family

- Porch time with our friends

- Sydney's endless craft projects at the table

- Dinner with neighbors

- Actual phone calls. Remember these? Instead of texting, you use your voice!

- I got four books read and had a fifth picked out.

- I even got to witness Caleb's new-at-the-time obsession with fishing

Don't these activities sound like fun ways to spend your afternoon? These activities don't have to be relegated to a by-gone black-and-white era; we can take control of our time again, of our thoughts, our words, our families, and create memories together in real life. Here are some great ideas to get you started. I'd love to hear how you choose to reconnect with yourself, your life, and your family and friends!

- SOME OF YOU ARE GOING TO THINK I've lost my mind for even suggesting this one, but here goes. "Perfect" family Christmas photo card? Give yourself, and your family, a year off. We know your kids fought you tooth and nail for two hours, and you likely screamed at someone so loud St. Nick heard you at the North Pole, just to be on someone's fridge with smiles we know you really had to work hard to produce. It's okay to take a breath. Grab those generic dollar store cards and tell your kids they get an extra two hours of playtime that day instead of posing for pictures.

- PICK OUT THOSE SOCIAL MEDIA OUTLETS most likely to fuel your need to do/buy/send/post more, and give those a rest for 7 days. Try and pick seven days for your break from these outlets that will add some peace to your holiday season and reduce that burden to overachieve.

- CREATE A SPOTIFY PLAYLIST with seven favorite Christmas songs that reflect the real reason for the season. Share your playlist with family and friends as a way to focus on everything you have to celebrate.

- DO YOU LOVE HOLIDAY MOVIES? Me too! Pick seven favorite Christmas movies and create a Family Night In to watch each one.

- IF YOU HAVE THE TIME and some musical inclination, take the Spotify list from above, and go sing those Christmas carols in your neighborhood or at an assisted living or nursing facility. Or help organize this one with your kids and some of their friends.

JEN'S

HOLIDAY

DIAL·IT·DOWN

FROM THE SOCIALS

Christmas 2011

So my little family said, God, if too much stuff is standing in the way of your kingdom coming in our lives, then help us break up with it. If it has stolen our allegiance and hijacked our obedience, give us the courage to wage war against everything that is ruining us for your gospel, substituting comfort for bravery, acquiring for sharing, appearances for obedience, personal glory for worship.

COMFORT FOR

Bravery,

ACQUIRING

for Sharing,

APPEARANCES FOR

Obedience,

PERSONAL GLORY FOR

Worship.

Reflections on Generosity

Is it really ground breaking news that too much media is bad for us? Is anyone thinking, *You know what my kids need? More TV.* I see couples having dinner in silence, checking their phones, as if *anything* cannot wait one hour. Don't get me started on the Bluetooth guy; it makes me want to ask, "Have you always been a jerk?" Wear it in the car, dude; do not wear it into Jason's Deli and have a loud conversation while making the cashier wait for your order. If I am close enough, I will pinch you, and I don't even know you.

Lots of experts are weighing in. It turns out, all this input isn't just annoying; it's troubling. A recent *New*

York Times article, citing dozens of sources, reported that *this is your brain on computers*:

> Scientists say juggling e-mail, phone calls and other incoming information can change how people think and behave. They say our ability to focus is being undermined by bursts of information.
>
> These play to a primitive impulse to respond to immediate opportunities and threats. The stimulation provokes excitement—a dopamine squirt—that researchers say can be addictive. In its absence, people feel bored. The resulting distractions can have deadly consequences, as when cell phone-wielding drivers and train engineers cause wrecks. And for millions of people these urges can inflict nicks and cuts on creativity and deep thought, interrupting work and family life.[1]

Even after this multitasking ends, fractured thinking persists because evidently *this is also your brain off computers.*

In 2008, people consumed three times more information each day than they did in 1960. New research shows computer users at work change windows, check e-mail, or switch programs nearly thirty-seven times an hour. I am completely guilty of this, and it gives me ping-pong brain. It is increasingly hard to focus on one task for longer than twenty minutes without succumbing to an alternate source: Hey look, my inbox says "6," my favorite blogger posted something new, let me just send this quick text, what's the daily recipe on cooks.com?

Researchers at Stanford found that media multitaskers seem more sensitive to incoming information than non-multitaskers, and that is not necessarily good:

A portion of the brain acts as a control tower, helping a person focus and set priorities. More primitive parts of the brain, like those that process sight and sound, demand that it pay attention to new information, bombarding the control tower when they are stimulated.

Researchers say there is an evolutionary rationale for the pressure this barrage puts on the brain. The lower-brain functions alert humans to danger, like a nearby lion, overriding goals like building a hut. In the modern world, the chime of incoming e-mail can override the goal of writing a business plan or playing catch with the children.

"Throughout evolutionary history, a big surprise would get everyone's brain thinking," said Clifford Nass, a communications professor at Stanford. "But we've got a large and growing group of people who think the slightest hint that something interesting might be going on is like catnip. They can't ignore it."[2]

The way I see it, if our brain needs attention, maybe there are better ways to meet that need. What if we gave our kids and our family the "Gift of Attention" this year? Instead of media distractions, I bet we can

find ways this holiday season to give our undivided attention to whomever God puts in front of us.

Try giving each kid at least fifteen minutes of undivided attention a day. Or, be open to a heavenly surprise! Who does Jesus want us to focus our generosity on today? While fifteen minutes may not sound like a lot of time, it's absolutely enough time to make someone feel seen, heard, and valued.

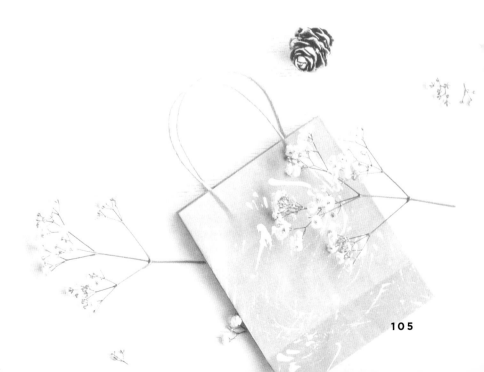

Final Thoughts

"So then, with endurance, let's also run the race that is laid out in front of us, since we have such a great cloud of witnesses surrounding us. Let's throw off any extra baggage, get rid of the sin that trips us up, and fix our eyes on Jesus, faith's pioneer and perfecter. He endured the cross, ignoring the shame, for the sake of the joy that was laid out in front of him, and sat down at the right side of the God's throne."

—HEBREWS 12:1-3

The month I gave up social media was heaven on a biscuit. 7 gave me permission to say, "Don't text me, don't Facebook me, and don't e-mail me unless it's an emergency because I won't answer." Can you ever imagine!? And then everything went silent.

As it turns out, I can set media boundaries and everyone will live. The instinct to check all my accounts and programs went dormant after a few anxious days of being certain that everyone else's lives were falling apart, because I wasn't talking to them. After day three, I was like an addict taking my first deep breath of unpoisoned air in a while. It was glorious!

I'm aware that the holidays might be the worst time (or could they be the best?) to put a dimmer on social media and screen time in general, but I don't want to be addicted anymore, and I certainly don't want my kids to be slaves to these compulsions. Instead of feeling stuck to a screen, I'd really rather be able to celebrate the season with those I love, in person, with words, and hugs, and tasty food, remembering the Reason we have all these blessings in the first place.

"Jesus replied, 'It's written,
People won't live only by bread.'"

—LUKE 4:4

LET US QUIET OUR MINDS
ENOUGH SO THAT WE CAN HEAR
THE WORD OF GOD AND SEE THE

Face of God

IN OUR CONVERSATIONS AND
INTERACTIONS WITH OTHERS.

FIVE

Tossing

". . . a woman came to him with a vase made of alabaster containing very expensive perfume. She poured it on Jesus' head while he was sitting at dinner."

—MATTHEW 26:7

5

Waste Not Want Not . . . As Much

We have so freaking much. So much money, education, resources, opportunities, knowledge, possessions, gifts, consumer power, privileges, advantages. We have every tool at our disposal, yet we are chronically plagued by ailments—social, spiritual, physical, and emotional. And we produce so . . . much . . . waste!

How many times have you bought a ton of veggies at the store, determined to eat them all *this time*, and then a week or four later you had to mop their stinky, liquefied remnants out of the veggie drawer in the refrigerator? Nobody? Just me then. Ooookay.

You might be more diligent with your groceries (and vegetable consumption) than I am, but I'm guessing there are a few areas of your life where you could be a little better about reducing the amount of waste you use, and, in turn, practicing ways to care for Creation.

But, of course, I'm not talking about *just* the food we waste. We waste money, time, natural resources, opportunities, material goods, brain cells . . . when we could be a little more intentional about what we use, and how often we use it. Brain cells included. I don't know about you but I need all of mine to function just to make it to the kitchen every morning. Coffee first. Fully functioning human second.

Joking aside, did you know that the U.S. has 3,091 active landfills and more than ten thousand old municipal landfills? Some cities are literally built on heaps of trash! The environmental issues these generate run the gamut from hazardous waste, toxic gas emissions, low-level radioactive waste, and leakage into ground and surface water. The health hazards posed cause much protestation and controversy.

Then there is the issue of volume, which even the most sophisticated system (and ours is pretty fancy) can handle for only so long. "Americans generate trash at an astonishing rate of 4.6 pounds per day per person, 251 million tons per year."[1] This is twice as much trash per person as most other developed countries. Trash production has almost tripled since 1960, thanks to the onslaught of prepackaged everything-under-the-sun.

Trash in a landfill will stay there, as is, for a super long time. Trash is dumped in sections (called cells), compacted, and covered with dirt before the next round. With little oxygen and moisture, trash does not decompose rapidly, as landfills aren't meant to break down trash, only bury it. When a landfill closes—because no site can bury trash indefinitely—it must be monitored for thirty years because of the contamination threat.

This is an unprecedented problem as ours is the first society to generate disposable material by the millions of tons annually. Plastic bottles, containers and packaging, technology waste . . . these are the byproducts of "modern progress." Cheese didn't always come packaged in plastic with paper dividers; people used to just make their own and then eat it. Mind blown.

Twenty-five years ago you'd be hard pressed to find a bottle of water for sale, but thanks to a clever industry who repackaged basic tap water and sold it to a society of convenience as a superior option, as if they collected it from the runoff of the Colorado Rockies, we now consume 8.6 million gallons of bottled water a year, at only a wee cost increase of 240 to 10,000 times the price of tap water.[2] Then into the trash, la de da. For the bargain price of a dollar, I receive sixteen ounces of tap water and contribute to the waste crisis.

But just when I was feeling tickled pink about recycling, I read this:

The most effective way to stop this trend is by preventing waste in the first place. . . . Waste is not just created when consumers throw items away. Throughout the life cycle of a product, from extraction of raw materials to transportation to processing and manufacturing facilities to manufacture and use, waste is generated. Reusing items or making them with less material decreases waste dramatically. Ultimately, less materials will need to be recycled or sent to landfills or waste combustion facilities.[3]

In other words, by the time I put my glass in the recycling bin, it has already caused the lion's share of damage by processing and shipping. Well, shoot! I was about to congratulate myself.

So, instead, dear reader, I say—*enough*.

Enough with the obscene excess while the rest of the world is burning down outside our windows. Enough with the waste as 25,000 people die today of hunger, while I throw away another pound of food we didn't get around to eating. Enough with the debt, the spending, the amassing, the irresponsibility, the indulgence, the fake discipleship, the rat race, the hamster wheel, the power and positioning and posturing with a hunger still for more, more, more, all the while pretending to follow a Jesus who didn't even have a place to lay His head.

True reform involves purchasing fewer disposable materials in the first place, like purchasing bulk products, produce from the farmer's market, and second-hand goods that have already shed their packaging. Best practices include reusing containers over and over and lowering the consumption of single-use materials. Recycling is probably a third-tier tactic toward genuinely reducing waste for maximum impact. But it is still totally worthwhile, so break those boxes down, separate the plastics, and drive the glass containers to the correct recycling bins across town, if you have to.

For the love of Pete, it's such a battle to be human, love Earth, and love Jesus well, isn't it? Especially during the holiday season! What would He think about all our Christmas decorations anyway? I'm guessing He'd roll His eyes at the massive amounts of wrapping paper and bows that I work so hard to use (and purchase and store, along with six more *new* tubes of paper) each year.

Look, I've watched the kids have gift-opening fatigue, slinking off upstairs to play with the couple of things they really cared about, and hoping we grownups won't call them back down to open up anything else. This is not normal. This is not healthy. They don't need *more stuff*. Neither do we.

Because guess what? Jesus is always enough, and He doesn't care about wrapping paper.

Favorites

For this round of the 7 Holiday Extravaganza, I'm giving you a mission to complete. Homework, if you will. No, no . . . don't roll your eyes. It'll be fun! It includes holiday shopping and eating locally in your own neighborhood. That's right! You can tell your friends that Jen Hatmaker told you to take a week or two to explore the cool restaurants and shops in your own little neighborhood (within five miles of your front door would be preferable, if you can swing it). Not only does this foster a sense of community and encourage green habits, you might meet some really neat neighbors. And I bet you'll find some great local stores you never knew existed!

To help reduce waste, remember to BYOB (bring your own bags) to the stores, and if you're daring enough . . . bring your own Tupperware with you to restaurants for leftovers. No, I'm not crazy to suggest such a thing. It doesn't make any sense to put perfectly good food in a container—even if it's recyclable—if we're just going to throw it away once we heat up the leftovers.

Below are some other ideas for how you can make a dent on waste in your corner of the world.

- AS IF YOU NEEDED ANOTHER REASON to visit your local farmer's market (do you, really?), this is a great place to get organic, non-packaged or minimally packages items, from local producers. It might even help you find new foods to try and prepare. The farmer's market is also a great place to buy gifts that don't require wrapping!

- IF YOU'VE TRADITIONALLY BEEN in a family where everything under the tree gets wrapped, even "Santa" gifts, talk to your family about having at least seven unwrapped gifts this year.

- GIVE SEVEN GIFTS THAT WILL ENCOURAGE WASTE REDUCTION or re-usability over disposability. For instance, give a refillable water bottle to your kids, who are (most likely) using disposable bottled water.

- CHOOSE A HOLIDAY GATHERING where the group usually uses disposable cups and plates, and offer to do the dishes as a family to save on that level of waste and as an act of service.

- CHOOSE SEVEN GIFTS TO GIVE THAT NEITHER GENERATE NOR PRODUCE ANY WASTE. It could be an article of clothing free of packaging, a gift of food given in a re-usable container, or a gift of service or time.

Christmas 2011

For some time, I've had this feeling messing with my faith. That one when you're trying really hard and adhering to most of the rules and checking a lot of boxes, I mean, some boxes that seem really important, legit boxes, and yet...I don't know. Something feels wrong. The mechanism is off. The parts are not creating the whole like people said it would. And despite my best efforts to kick that self-condemnation thing, I can't help but think:

To the other 99 percent, it's probably obvious, but for me in my privileged 1 percent demographic, it left me puzzled and frustrated and discouraged. A bunch of my generation, millions if you want to get nitpicky, up and left the church over it, because the template didn't end up changing the world or even changing lives. It left us with a laundry list of behaviors but conspicuously ignored way too many elephants in the room to be taken seriously. For me, the tension had many facets:

Why are we still starving for nourishment after our sixth Bible study in a row? How can people supposedly filled with the Spirit be so enamored with the luxuries of this world to the detriment of the other 99 percent who suffer so? How can the richest people on earth still be so unhappy? Does my craving for more neutralize the enough that Jesus says He is? If I'm patterned after my Savior, why does my life look exactly like everyone else's, with the exception of some stellar church attendance? The tension finally pinpointed here:

As believers in the western church, how can we have so much and do so little with it?

HOW CAN WE

Have So Much

AND

Do So Little

WITH IT?

Reflections on Generosity

If you haven't figured it out yet, let me tell you something: We Hatmakers are wasters. We are consumers. We are definitely a part of the problem. I no more think about how my consumption affects the earth or anyone else living on it than I think about becoming a personal trainer; there is just no category for it in my mind.

So for this month, I choose seven habits for a greener life:

- Gardening

- Composting

- Conserving energy and water

- Recycling (everything, all of it)

- Driving only one car (for the love of the land)

- Shopping thrift and second-hand

- Buying only local

If you've implemented these habits for years, forgive me if I ever called you *earthy crunchy*. We originally did none of these, so this was a giant departure from careless consumption that requires nothing of me.

But you know what? I really grew to enjoy most of these challenges. In fact, gardening and composting have been both fun and life-giving in more ways than one. I've been thrilled with just how much our back yard can produce when tended with care (and watered regularly) by The Karpophore Project (pronounced car-puh-fuh-RAY-oh), a Greek word that means "to bear fruit in every good work." The KP Project bears genuine fruit, from the soil and in the lives of real people. This is their mission:

> The Karpophore Project bears real fruit (and vegetables and farm-fresh products!) in the truly good work of

reclaiming our barren and underutilized landscapes. We aim to be a blessing to the environment, to the social fabric, and to the lives of beautiful people across the city of Austin.

First of all, I love people. I especially love people who are passionate about what they do—even better when it helps others. And I love being able to have fresh vegetables whenever I want and to be able to donate the rest to people who would otherwise not have access to fresh, organic veggies. It's truly a win-win!

As for the composting, it's just cool. What can I say? Being able to watch leftover food scraps turn into nutrient-rich dirt, to then continue the cycle and circle of life as it becomes yummy food . . . it's about as close to a *Lion King* moment as there's ever going to be in my back yard. And I promise you, the next time I hold up a giant cucumber I've just plucked from the vine, I'm going to thrust it toward the sun like it's a newborn lion cub and christen it Simba. So there.

Final Thoughts

"The earth is the Lord's and everything in it,
the world and its inhabitants too.
Because God is the one who established it on
the seas; God set it firmly on the waters."

—PSALM 24:1-2

If you're feeling a little overwhelmed at the thought of how much waste we produce—especially in the name of Christmas—don't let it put you in a Bah-Humbug mood this year. Instead, think about all of the opportunities you now have to practice green habits like recycling, reusing, or regifting with minimal packaging!

I know we might see the great big world around us and assume there are an infinite amount of resources for our every need, but that's not true. "There is not always more. Except for our energy income from the sun, the world is finite. Numbers of individual organisms may seem limitless, but they are not. Species may appear to be beyond counting, but they are finite in number. Our life support systems may seem beyond abuse, but there are limits to what they can bear. Like it or not, we are finite creatures living in a finite world."[4]

As certainly as God created man in His image, He first created the earth. With the same care He designed sixty thousand miles of blood vessels in the human body, He also crafted hydrangeas and freshwater rapids and hummingbirds. He balanced healthy ecosystems with precision and established climates and beauty. He integrated colors and smells and sounds that would astound humanity. The details He included while designing the earth are so extraordinary, it is no wonder He spent five of the six days of creation on it.

So why don't we care for the earth anywhere near to the degree we do our bodies? Why don't we fuss and examine and steward creation with the same tenacity? Why aren't we refusing complicity in the ravaging of our planet? Why aren't we determined to stop pillaging the earth's resources like savages? Why do we mock environmentalists and undermine their passion for conservation? Do we think ourselves so superior to the rest of creation that we are willing to deplete the earth to supply our luxuries? If so, we may very well be the last generation who gets that prerogative.

I've been gobbling up the goodies, making a huge mess, and assuming someone else would clean it up and foot the bill. But let me tell you, this month put the brakes on that. I cannot believe how God has captured me for creation care. All of it: recycling, using less, gardening, composting, conserving, buying local, repurposing instead of replacing; I'm in. From the nearly empty garbage bin to the lower electric bill, the immediate effects of a greener lifestyle are obvious.

My land, do we have far to go! My hypocrisies are too numerous to count, but this month birthed something unmistakable: I'm done separating ecology from theology, pretending they don't originate from the same source.

A friend said, "I don't know why you're trying. It won't matter. No one else cares." To that, I'll close with this bit of wisdom:

> If God is really at the center of things and God's
> good future is the most certain reality, then the truly
> realistic course of action is to buck the dominant
> consequentialist ethic of our age—which says that
> we should act only if our action will most likely bring
> about good consequences—and simply, because we
> are people who embody the virtue of hope, do the
> right thing. If we believe it is part of our task as earth
> keepers to recycle, then we ought to recycle, whether
> or not it will change the world. Do the right
> thing. If we think it part and parcel of our

ecological obedience to drive less and walk more, then
that is what we ought to do. Do the right thing. We
should fulfill our calling to be caretakers of the earth
regardless of whether global warming is real or there
are holes in the ozone layer or three nonhuman species
become extinct each day. Our vocation is not contingent
on results or the state of the planet. Our calling simply
depends on our identity as God's response-able human
image-bearers.[5]

GOD CARES.

I CARE.

Let's Do The Right Thing.

SIX

Spending

"We were once foolish, disobedient, deceived, and slaves to our desires and various pleasures too."

—TITUS 3:3

6

We're Not Made of Money

I'm dying to rediscover what is simple and magnificent about the Savior of the World coming to Earth, putting on flesh and saving my life. I so want my kids to marvel that Jesus came, just like God said He would, and He split history in two, forever transforming the concepts of hope and peace and salvation. And I just feel like when I create a season revolving around wish lists, frenzy, and alternate characters of honor, my kids will never understand any of this.

Remember when you were a little round-faced kid with your mom or dad in the store and you saw something you just had to have or it was going to absolutely be the end of the world, so you begged and pleaded and teetered on the verge of a public tantrum, but no amount of pouty face could change their mind? Your dad probably offered some rendition of the famous parental rebuttal: "Money doesn't grow on trees." Or "Do I look like I'm made of money?" Well, turns out they were right. Dagnabbit.

I mean, I'm certain you've figured this out by now though. What with school and a career and bills and maybe a business or a family. We work our buns off to make ends meet and afford a certain lifestyle—whatever that consists of—so shouldn't we pay more attention to how and where we spend our money?

Yes. Yes, we should.

Now, I don't know what your situation may be—you could have a sky's-the-limit budget, or you might be worried about getting by this holiday season. In either case, there is real pressure here, folks.

First of all who came up with the idea that we're supposed to check items off the list, and we're now trading spreadsheets in Google Drive and demanding our kids send urls to the exact product pages if they don't want to be disappointed?

Half the time, the kids don't even want *the toy*. They'd rather we give them our time or give them a break, or give ourselves one so we're not quite so cranky this time of year.

There's also this thing with families out there— surely not yours or mine, right?—that have some level of dysfunction around either money or Christmas, which usually leads to craziness around the combination of the two. We often feel burdened to overspend to make sure everyone gets what they want. For many of us, that leads to months of stress and paying off debt after the holiday is over. And that's not fun for anyone!

There's pressure to buy for this cousin or that friend or coworker, not to slight anyone, or to make sure Santa's gifts don't look paltry next to the grandparents' gifts. The list of guilt and shame angles around holiday spending goes on and on. And so every season, we march right in, saying we're going to scale it back but never do.

The aftermath begins in January, when the credit card bill arrives. This is not the celebration of His birthday that our Jesus had in mind for us. It's just not. So we decided to change it up and be more aware of what we spent money on and where.

Now, we went hardcore and decided on only seven vendors where we were spending our money during this part of the experiment. They were:

- The Sunset Valley Farmer's Market

- HEB gas station (flex fuel!)

- Online bill pay

- Kids' school

- Limited travel fund

- Emergency medical

- Target

But of course, you can choose whichever stores you'd like. The key is to make note of how often you go shopping or eat out. Can you consolidate any errands? Can you eat at home more nights than normal? And how much money can you save if you only get the items on your shopping list—the items you actually *need* to buy, instead of all the items you want to buy?

If you practice this consistently, whether over a few weeks or a few months, you will absolutely save money. Maybe hundreds. Potentially thousands. And you'll be proud of yourself for creating a new, healthy habit.

So good for you! This deserves a celebration. And not of the financial kind. Tonight, make sure you celebrate while sitting down to a delicious meal you cooked, and think about all the money you'll be saving for something really special someday—your future!

Favorites

Saving money is something most people aspire to do, especially during the holidays, and it can be a little harder than it seems—but only at first! Once you have a handle on what you spend each month and where, you can easily see areas where you can pull back a bit. So, here are some ideas to help get you started on being master over your money, instead of the other way around.

- PICK OUT SEVEN GIFTS that you can give that do not cost money. Spread these out between your family, your neighbor, your community, and someone you don't know.

- TALK TO YOUR FAMILY, at least your immediate family, about spending less money on presents and more time focused on showing generosity in other ways. Work together to flat-out mark some items off of the wish lists.

- PICK SEVEN CHARITABLE ORGANIZATIONS that your family cares about, and give donations to those charities as part of your Christmas wish list.

- THIS COULD PROVE TO BE COMPLETELY IMPOSSIBLE, given your situation, but see if you can limit your holiday shopping to seven trips out and to only seven places. Consolidate the online orders and excursions, and see if doing so will free up some time.

- WORK WITH YOUR FAMILY to plan time to spend together, instead of money, and make plans for seven activities with your family unit that allow you to give time as a gift to those around you. It could be switching out a shopping day for an afternoon with a friend, or inviting Grandma over for a gingerbread house-building competition with the kids. Use these moments to be the Jesus we're celebrating in the world.

Christmas 2015

During a month when the TV tells us to buy someone a Lexus and put a bow on it (because America), I can't help but link Advent and Jesus to the great hope of all nations. He came. Just like He said He would. And He made salvation available to the whole world. He went well outside His own borders and invited us all into the greatest story ever told.

I just paid my son $50 to take down/pack up all of Christmas. Worst thing you ever heard or THE SMARTEST?

JESUS PRAYED THAT
WE WOULD
Become One
WITH EACH OTHER, AND
BECOMING ONE MEANS WHAT
IS
Good For Us
IS
Good For All
AND WHAT OPPRESSES ONE
OPPRESSES ALL.

Reflections on Generosity

One night, towards the end of the 7 experiment, while our friends went to dinner, the kids and I drove home, as we weren't spending money in restaurants that month, talking about 7 and struggling through the concept of self-denial. My kids' generation has never been told "no." This is a hard sell. Not quite old enough to grasp obedience to Jesus in a self-serving culture, we listed the tangible results of 7 so far, including:

- We are eating 100 percent healthier.

- We gave a ton of stuff to people who had nothing.

- We maintained several reforms from media month.

- Our carbon footprint is cut in half.

- We learned to garden, and we love it.

- We've pared down our rooms, our drawers, our closets, our stuff.

- We're thinking about, praying for, sharing with, and spending time with marginalized people.

- We sponsored a new child through Help End Local Poverty with money we reallocated.

- Lots of our friends have joined us.

- Our prayers are changing.

We came up with this list and then some, culling lessons out of 7 thus far. We talked about how fasting helps us think differently. I validated their sadness at missing dinner, telling them my hardest 7 moments, too.

As usual, Sydney was most engaged, my spiritually sensitive bleeding-heart child. She will live in Haiti or adopt ten children or translate the Bible into an obscure language one day. She carries her emotions close, and they leak out at the slightest provocation. She thinks deeply. She cares sincerely. She worries about homeless people on cold nights. She cries over dead squirrels (well, he should have looked both ways).

Then, there are my boys. I desperately worry they'll have to provide for a family someday. Where thoughts on Scripture and life aspirations reside in Sydney's brain, there is a black hole for the boys, crowded out by football and Nintendo and whatever is shiny in front of their faces. I can hold them in deep territory for about forty-three seconds.

After a twenty-minute discussion on fasting, I noticed all three kids staring pensively out the window, thinking their thoughts. I decided to mine their conclusions to show my readers how well I parented through this experiment. "Hey guys? Whatcha thinking?"

Sydney: You know? We only missed one dinner out with friends. Big deal. Think how many meals the homeless people miss, Mom. Instead of feeling sorry for myself, I'm going to think about them tonight. At least we have a home to go to and food in our kitchen to eat.

Caleb: Mom? If I had to pick a superpower, I would teleport.

Awesome.

Final Thoughts

"But your loyal love, Lord, extends to the skies; your faithfulness reaches the clouds. Your righteousness is like the strongest mountains; your justice is like the deepest sea. Lord, you save both humans and animals. Your faithful love is priceless, God! Humanity finds refuge in the shadow of your wings. They feast on the bounty of your house; you let them drink from your river of pure joy. Within you is the spring of life. In your light, we see light."

—PSALM 36:5-9

We spend a lot of money. Combing through a year of bank statements, we are not big-ticket item buyers; we nickel and dime ourselves to death. We spend almost everything we make, and honestly, I can barely account for half of it.

This is why spending has flown under my radar; it is subtle, incremental, and seemingly inconsequential. Just this little thing here and that small thing there. I don't feel like cooking; let's just get this. Individually, nothing too egregious, but together our spending amounts to a startling number.

Big deal, right? Do I really need to care about this high-end lipstick? Does it actually hurt someone if I buy these jeans or help someone if I don't? Let's say I cut spending down and work toward less consumption. So what? Is there even a chance my choices would matter?

I think they might. In fact, I see three easy shifts we could make, starting today:

One, nonconsumption.

This is the simplest and hardest. It takes true courage to rage against this machine. Could we be countercultural enough to say, "We're not buying that. We don't need that. We'll make do with what we have. We'll use the stuff we already own." If this causes anxiety, I'm with you, trust me. Because who else does that? Who curbs their appetites anymore? Who uses old stuff when they could buy new stuff? Who sews patches on jeans or uses last year's backpacks? Who says "no" when they can afford to say "yes"?

We could. We could wisely discern needs from wants, and frankly, at least half of those line items are misfiled. Let's take advice from Matthew Sleeth in *Serve God, Save the Planet*: "My grandmother has hundreds of axioms. One of them was 'If you think you want something, wait a month.' One of three things will happen if you follow this sage advice. One: You will forget. Two: You will no longer need it. Or three: You will need it more. Most often, numbers one and two will happen."[1]

We can simply stop spending so much, use what we have, borrow what we need, repurpose possessions instead of replacing them, and—the kicker—live with less. Like Barber noted, "The challenge is to demonstrate that as consumers we can know what we want and want only what we need; and that, with the rest of our lives we intend to live as lovers or artists or learners or citizens in a plethora of life worlds in which consumption need play no role."[2]

Two, redirect all that money saved.

Humor me: What if we lived on 75 percent of our income and gave the rest away strategically? Or what if we downsized to 50 percent, bringing fresh meaning to Jesus' command to "love our neighbor as ourselves." Pulling out of a lopsided market is one thing; redistributing wealth to the world's vulnerable is a whole'nother level. Global microlending, anyone? Go to www.kiva.org to learn about microfinancing for small businesses, for as little as $25. There is a 98 percent repayment rate. Astonishing. Empowering indigenous people to transform their own communities is the most effective weapon against global poverty.

Your giving can effect extraordinary change. Pick a need, country, group of people, an organization focused

on empowerment and sustainable independence. You could be an answer to countless prayers. The poor don't lack ambition, imagination, or intelligence; most simply lack resources. We have what they require and more than we need. We could share.

Three, become wiser consumers.

I talked in 7 about supporting vendors who take a strong stand on human rights issues, like sustainability.

With watchdog groups like Not For Sale, change.org, free2work.org, and others, we have the ability to choose our vendors and learn more about companies that are doing good socially.

Plus, sometimes all it takes is a little creativity to be more conscious consumers and better gift givers. After we completed 7, we changed our Christmas gift structure, because before it was just absolute pandemonium . . . I mean, too much stuff for a bunch of kids who didn't even want half of it. Of course, they just ripped through it like *Lord of the Flies*, and one week later we didn't know where half of it was, or what we even bought, and they were playing with exactly one-tenth of it all. So we implemented a Christmas structure for each kid: "something you want, something you need, something to wear, something to read," and that was their gift. It made everything feel much more manageable. I felt like I got

Christmas back without all the stress and pressure of it all. Once the kids knew what to expect, we had a great time.

I learned another fantastic gift-giving idea from my mother-in-law. Instead of giving physical presents for Christmas or birthdays, she would give the gift of an experience. Each kid would have a whole day, one-on-one with grandma, to do whatever they wanted (within reason). She did all kinds of stuff with them—plays, vacations, movies, you name it—and they'll never forget those special experiences.

I know that it is easy to become paralyzed by the world's suffering and the inequalities created by corruption and greed. There's so much to be done and we are only one person with a limited number of hours in each day and limited resources. But we actually hold *immense power* for change, simply by virtue of our wealth and economic independence. Because we decide where our dollars go and where our time is spent. Never has so much wealth been so concentrated; our prosperity is unprecedented. If enough of us decided to share, we would unleash a torrent of justice to sweep away disparity, extreme poverty, and hopelessness.

The world is waiting. Our kids are watching. Time is wasting.

Are we willing?

IF ENOUGH OF US

DECIDED TO SHARE,

WE WOULD UNLEASH A

Torrent of Justice

TO SWEEP AWAY DISPARITY,

EXTREME POVERTY, AND

HOPELESSNESS.

SEVEN

Stressing

"They went quickly and found Mary and Joseph, and the baby lying in the manger. When they saw this, they reported what they had been told about this child. Everyone who heard it was amazed at what the shepherds told them. Mary committed these things to memory and considered them carefully. The shepherds returned home, glorifying and praising God for all they had heard and seen. Everything happened just as they had been told."

—LUKE 2:16-20

7

Blessed and Still Stressed?

A quick word for those about to spend time with difficult people, or polar opposite family members, or those whose views break your heart or boggle your mind, or mean, judgey, or passive aggressive types: Christmas does not represent your one moment to "set them straight" or challenge their ideas or go on record or finally get through. Nor does it mean you bend over backward, explain your choices, cower to criticism, or take the bait. (The bait never works. I always regret taking it. The only thing at the end is a skewered fish.)

Just lay all that down. Release your anxiety and just let these days be what they are: Christmas Eve and Christmas Day with the family you have. You choose how much control you will hand over. None of this will be perfect. Consider the expectations you are entertaining: too high? Maybe unrealistic? Are you hoping someone acts differently than they *always have*?

As much as it depends on you, steer your own ship. No, I will not jump into this never-ending argument. No, I will not explain to Aunt Margaret why we put our kids in public school. No, I will not feed off my mother's disappointment. No, I will not pick a fight. No, I will not bring up that one thing nor respond to someone else resurrecting old wounds. No, I will not answer grandpa's nosy questions about my dating life/marriage/salary/divorce/struggling kid.

For many, your next days will be easy, but for those of you walking into stressful scenarios, take your expectations down to the ground, then anything above that is a bonus! Let it be what it is. YOU can add kind words, generous responses, positive intent, and good jokes into the mix. You can up the ante on joy. You can shrug things off instead of going up in flames. You can complement instead of criticize. You can walk outside and take a deep breath (bring your eggnog). You can be the best thing happening in the room.

We're being encouraged to be generous with our grace and our time and our words. If we are gracious toward other people, it's hard to be stressed about them. And that extends, too, to giving room for surprises and messed-up surprises and things not going just as planned.

Plus, I'm pretty sure if I told you that your goal should be to avoid all stress during the Christmas season, first you'd do a laugh-and-roll-your-eyes combo, and next you'd want to slap me. But since I don't love being slapped, instead I'll tell you that if you can manage to avoid any of the typical anxiety-producing situations that accompany holidays, you get an A+. Bonus points if you are able to create some kind of self-care routine that helps you stay sane and focus on what really matters this time of year—JESUS. Naps and massages tie for a close second.

I mean, think about it. Isn't it silly that we put soooooo much effort, money, time, and emotion into celebrating Christmas? Don't get me wrong—our Lord and Savior deserves every bit of it and then some. But I'm also pretty sure He never intended for His birthday to turn into a materialistic holiday to see who has the coolest toys, spending money we don't have, and doing things we don't want with people we don't like (sometimes). *We're kind of missing the point, guys. Big time.*

I also really wonder what He thinks about His likeness and other holy symbols being turned into chocolate candy. Weird flex, right? Cue Tommy grabbing a chocolate cross from his Christmas stocking. "Mmmm!" He beams, a bit of chocolate melts on his chubby fingers as he hastily unwraps the treat. He takes a bite and discovers a texture much like a chocolate-covered Rice Krispy treat and giggles. "I like crunchy Jesus!" *Sigh*. This is not what God intended.

Anyway. So yes, I'm certain that your calendar will probably be the busiest it's ever been right around Christmas. And you have expectations you've set for yourself (or that you've accepted from others) to buy gifts, make food, do all the things, be nice to all the people, and be all places at once. And that, my friend, is going to make you mis.er.a.ble.

With all that *doing* you're doing, where are you going to find the time for *being*? Wouldn't it be wonderful to spend some time each day in prayer and meditation? Would it be nice to have just a few moments each day to yourself, to think about what really matters? I'm not asking you to shut yourself away in your prayer closet for an hour each day (If you can do that, great!). But what if you observed a few pauses each day to remember the Holiest of Holies? Even if that's all you can do, that's enough. I promise.

God did not come to earth to stress us out. He did not grant us grace so that we might wallow in traffic, cursing under our breath at the idiot who didn't take advantage of the yellow light so we could make it to Uncle Joe's house exactly by 6:30 p.m.

He came to set us free.

Favorites

When we originally did 7, our family decided we'd observe seven sacred times each day to meditate and pray, to rest and to be rejuvenated. We used *Seven Sacred Pauses*, a book written by Macrina Wiederkehr, who is a member of the monastic community St. Scholastica. Her wisdom is so profound, I underlined nearly every sentence in the book. She describes the seven pauses as "breathing spells for the soul," an oasis to remember the sacredness of life, who we are, how to offer God the incredible gift of our lives, and learning to *be* in the midst of so much *doing*.[1] We paused and prayed seven times a day at these times:

The Night Watch (midnight)

The Awakening Hour (dawn)

The Blessing Hour (midmorning)

The Hour of Illumination (noon)

The Wisdom Hour (midafternoon)

The Twilight Hour (early evening)

The Great Silence (bedtime)

If seven separate times of reflection seem too much to begin with, at least consider adding two times of reflection into your day—morning (dawn) and evening (bedtime)—and see how that feels. If you can maintain those, add more. Pro tip: set a daily alarm on your phone to remind you of these times.

Now, you don't have to do any sacred chants or sit in a certain way or even pray a certain prayer. This is all about you being alone with God, resting in the silence of a peaceful moment, being thankful for each day, and hopefully reclaiming more of yourself and your schedule from the world.

- PICK UP A GIFT BOOK OR DEVOTIONAL on the Advent. Not saying you have to read the whole thing, but keep it in your bag or car or kitchen, and just sneak a peek at the beginning of the day, when you can. Grab those small in-between moments to throw a quick prayer up for Yuletide sanity.

- GIVE YOURSELF PERMISSION TO SAY NO to something you've said yes to in the past. Forget social pressures and norms and expectations. Pick one holiday gathering, one office party, or one distant relative's punch bowl invitation to say *no* to, and reclaim that time for yourself and your family to do something birth-of-Jesus related. Go to a nativity play, if you haven't before, or try that Christmas caroling I mentioned earlier.

- I KNOW IT SOUNDS LIKE IT WOULD GO WITHOUT SAYING, but read the Christmas story with your family or kids. It's amazing how easy it can be for that important ritual to get squeezed out of the season.

- AND WITH THAT, IN LINE WITH OUR PRAYERS AND MEDITATIONS IN 7, make a plan for meditating on the unbelievable truth of God as a baby in a manger. Find a few times this season to say, "Thank you, Jesus, for coming into this world." You might even get the lyrics to some of those Christmas songs to be a part of those meditations and prayers.

In addition to adding a few precious pauses into your daily routine, you can also consider upping your self-care game and it doesn't even have to cost you any money! Try these ideas:

- GIVE YOURSELF A MANICURE OR PEDICURE. Or, even better—a foot massage with that nice flowery lotion you bought but never use.

- TAKE 5-10 MINUTES TO DO SOME STRETCHING. Your body and mind will thank you, especially if you have an office job.

- IS IT NICE OUTSIDE? Make sure you have some sunscreen on and then go outside for a bit. Find a bench, a tree, a soft patch of grass, and just relax for a few minutes.

- DO YOU LIVE IN ONE OF THOSE LUCKY PLACES that actually has snow during the Christmas season? Throw a snowball! How long has it even been since you rolled a snowball or made a snowman? Even better, go sledding. Make hot chocolate—with marshmallows, obviously.

- IF YOU LIVE IN A WARMER CLIMATE, make yourself a picnic lunch with your favorite holiday foods and have a blast! Everyone else around you will be so jealous that they don't have a picnic lunch. You will be the talk of the town.

- WHAT IF THE WEATHER IS JUST PLAIN YUCKY? Celebrate anyway. Have a dance party in your kitchen; play music and sing all throughout your house; bake cookies and watch a feel-good Christmas movie. Finally put up your tree. Or don't. Whatever helps you destress and focus on the blessings around you.

JEN'S
HOLIDAY
DIAL·IT·DOWN

FROM THE SOCIALS

Christmas 2018

I love you, dear ones. Very proud of those of you creating the family you want while still connected to the family you got. I hope your days are surprisingly lovely, but even if they aren't, you are still deeply loved by Jesus, who had a challenging first "Christmas" too and still managed to save the world.

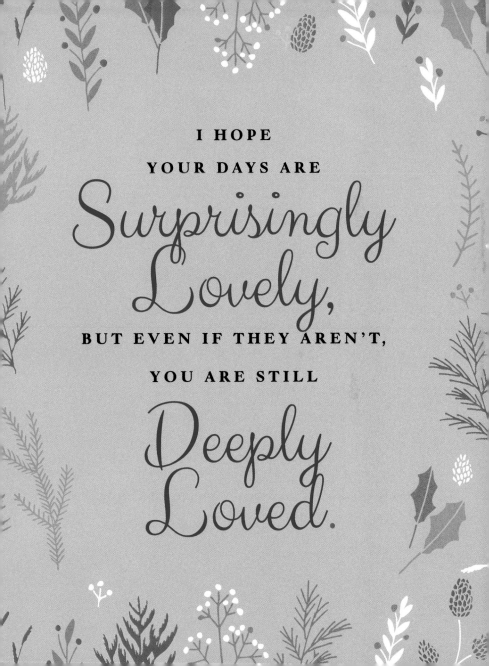

I HOPE
YOUR DAYS ARE
Surprisingly
Lovely,
BUT EVEN IF THEY AREN'T,
YOU ARE STILL
Deeply
Loved.

Reflections on Generosity

Want to hear an embarrassing story? Of course you do.

Brandon is unquestionably the gift giver in our family. It fits his skillset. It is his thing. It is what he loves to do. I am below average at best. So, unless I tell him, "I don't want you to get me anything or definitely nothing expensive," he will do it. Naturally, I have come to expect big gestures from him.

One Christmas, probably three years ago, I am in the kitchen making dinner, and he comes in with this big wrapped box, and I mean it is *big*. And it is obviously heavy. He looks at me like the cat who swallowed the canary because this is obviously my *big gift*, and he is really pleased.

I said, "Oh, my goodness, wow, somebody has been shopping. I sure hope it isn't pots and pans!" Ha, ha, ha . . . we laughed it out. Nobody says a thing.

The next morning, I am cooking breakfast, and I open my cabinets and inside are stacked the most beautiful set of copper pots and pans. *Crap!* He had gotten me copper pots and pans! I love food and cooking! But after I said, "Those better not be pots and pans," he went in that night and unboxed the whole thing and put them in my cabinet.

I felt soooo bad. *How do I keep ruining presents?* We still laugh about it—my terrible Jen moment. And I love those darn pots and pans.

As you can imagine, my takeaways from the 7 experiment have been so vast, I sometimes couldn't keep an idea still long enough to write about it. Swimming in my brain was the huge list of reforms with new habits and practices. Some of them we were able to maintain with decent regularity. Others seemed to fade out. And that's okay.

This was the beginning of a process for us, as it likely is for you—not a complete story by itself. Whatever God has done or is doing in our family is certainly not a template, and I don't want it to be. We live in a certain city with a certain task, we have specific gifts, and we're horribly deficient in others. Our life looks like it does because we are the Hatmakers, and God is dealing with us the way He's dealing with us. We have history and sin issues and circumstances and geography that God takes into account as He stakes our place in His kingdom.

You have an entirely different set of factors. I have no idea what this might look like in your life, nor do I want that job. Your story is God's to write, not mine. But I do have some takeaways from it all that I think are worth sharing. Maybe they'll resonate with you, too.

Love God most. Love your neighbor as yourself. This is everything.

If we say we love God, then we will care about the poor.

This earth is God's and everything in it. We should live like we believe this.

What we treasure reveals what we love.

Money and stuff have the power to ruin us.

Act justly, love mercy, walk humbly with God. This is what is required.

Final Thoughts

"Give thanks to the Lord because he is good.
God's faithful love lasts forever!"

—PSALM 136:1

Life is still crazy. But I still do my best to practice those seven sacred times each day to meditate and pray. I've found they do as much for my relationship with God as they so for my relationship with myself. The daily times of prayer and stillness have inspired me into deeper communion with God. The mindfulness has been terribly stretching. And the ability to prioritize those special times has helped me greatly to pause throughout the day and recalibrate my heart and mind.

I've also discovered that it takes *continued effort* to make those sacred times a priority. I can fast from clothes and waste and spending easier than I can fast from busyness. Wear the same outfit six days straight? Sure. Garden and recycle? No problem. Pause seven times a day in the middle of my life? *Geez*. What about setting aside a whole day to honor the Sabbath? Now that's asking a lot.

One of the most beautiful gifts we've been given is the Sabbath, and we still protect that day pretty fiercely. We observe it on Sundays, the only true day of rest in our weird life and weird schedule. Even so, I found this month very challenging and equally beautiful. Evidently, I don't respond well to scheduled interruptions, Spirit-led or otherwise.

But these pauses have taught me something: My heart craves a slower life. I want people to stop prefacing their phone calls with this: "I know you're

so busy, but if I could just have a second. . ." I want
to figure out what this means for our family. We can't
live in the barn forever, nor can we pull out of work,
ministry, school, community, mission, family, and all
the activities that accompany them. But what can we
do to cultivate a quiet ranch heart in a noisy urban
world?

As God explained at the inauguration of the Sabbath:

*Remember the Sabbath day and treat it as
holy. Six days you may work and do all your
tasks, but the seventh day is a Sabbath to the
Lord your God. Do not do any work—not
you, your sons or daughters, your male or
female servants, your animals,*

or the immigrant who is living with you. Because the Lord made the heavens and the earth, the sea, and everything that is in them in six days, but rested on the seventh day. That is why the Lord blessed the Sabbath day and made it holy.

—EXODUS 20:8-11

Is it coincidental that God named every person included in the rest? Sons and daughters, servers and animals, guests and visitors; we all need this. My neglect of the Sabbath doesn't just affect me but my entire household, my extended community. The pace we keep has jeopardized our health and happiness, our worship and rhythms. We belong to a culture that can't catch its breath; rather, we refuse to catch our breath.

God doesn't pull any punches here: The Sabbath is holy. Not lazy, not selfish, not unproductive; not helpful, not optional, not just a good idea. *Holy.* Like God demonstrated in Exodus 16, He'll provide for daily needs, but on the sixth day He'll rain down a double portion to store up for the Sabbath, covering our needs while we rest. The only day a double collection wouldn't spoil by dawn's light was the Sabbath; God made a way.

He still does. Originally, the Sabbath had to be planned for, food gathered a day in advance. It wasn't handed to the Hebrews on a silver platter. This principle remains. I still have to plan for the Sabbath, tying up loose ends and gathering what we'll need. I still have to prepare the family for rest, enforcing healthy boundaries and protecting our calendar. I still have to set work aside and trust in the wisdom of God's design. "Look! The Lord has given you the Sabbath" (Exodus 16:29).

My heart feels renewed at the completion of the month. Perhaps the greatest gift is clarity. My mission is concentrated: this matters, this doesn't, this counts, this doesn't. It's actually not that complicated. The Bible is true; no matter how contrary to reality it appears. I've discovered you can press extremely hard on the Word, and it will hold.

It *is* healing to forgive.

You *do* gain your life by losing it.

Love *does* truly conquer evil.

A simple life really *is* liberating.

As I wrap up these seven exercises, I'll quote a prayer written by Henri Nouwen, which resonates so deeply, it's as if he stole my thoughts:

> Dear Lord, you have sent me in to this world to preach your word. So often the problems of the world seem so complex and intricate that your

word strikes me as embarrassingly simple. Many times I fell tongue-tied in the company of people who are dealing with the world's social and economic problems.

But you, O Lord, said, "Be clever as serpents and innocent as doves." Let me retain innocence and simplicity in the midst of this complex world. I realize that I have to be informed, that I have to study the many aspects of the problems facing the world, and that I have to try to understand as well as possible the dynamics of our contemporary society. But what really counts is that all this information, knowledge, and insight allow me to speak more clearly and unambiguously your truthful word. Do not allow evil powers to seduce me with the complexities of the world's problems, but give me the strength to think clearly, speak freely, and act boldly in your service.[1]

GIVE ME THE COURAGE TO

Show the Dove

IN A WORLD OF

SERPENTS.

FINAL HOLIDAY THOUGHTS

"I bring you good news to you—wonderful,

joyous news for all people."

—LUKE 2:10

Christmas 2015

Good news.

Great joy.

All people.

It is the substance of our entire theology. How on earth we started outsourcing the idea that following Jesus was harsh and boring, that a life hidden in His ways was somber and hard,

and that faith was more about defending against
"outsiders" than throwing the doors open to every
beloved person, I have no idea.

But in a manger for the ordinary, not a palace for the
elite,

God brought us good news that caused great joy for
all people.

Thank you for coming, Jesus.

You have brought me such great joy.

You are my forever favorite.

MY FAVORITE SOURCES

CHAPTER 1: KITCHEN

1. Richard Rohr, *Simplicity* (New York: Crossroad Publishing Company, 2003), 99–100.

CHAPTER 3: STUFF

1. Richard Rohr, *Simplicity* (New York: Crossroad Publishing Company, 2003), 59–60.

CHAPTER 4: STREAMING

1. Richtel, Matt. "Hooked on Gadgets, and Paying a Mental Price." *The New York Times*, June 7, 2010.

2. Ibid.

CHAPTER 5: TOSSING

1. Freudenrich, Ph.D., Craig. "How Landfills Work." How Stuff Works. Last modified October 16, 2000.

2. McColgan, Cameron. "True cost ounce by ounce of water in 2012 (Bottled vs. Tap)." Dabble With…. Last modified April 11, 2012.

3. See http://www.epa.gov/epawaste/conserve/rrr/reduce.htm.

4. Steven Bouma-Prediger, *For the Beauty for the Earth: A Christian Vision for Creation Care* (Grand Rapids: Baker Academic, 2010), 20.

5. Ibid., 182

CHAPTER 6: SPENDING

1. J. Matthew Sleeth, *Serve God Save the Planet: A Christian Call to Action* (Grand Rapids: Zondervan, 2007), 83.

2. Benjamin R. Barber, *Consumed: How Markets Corrupt Children, Infantilize Adults, and Swallow Citizens Whole* (New York: WW Norton, 2007), 292.

CHAPTER 7: STRESSING

1. Henri Nouwen, *Seeds of Hope* (New York: Doubleday, 1997), 112.

ACKNOWLEDGEMENTS

The most heartfelt thanks to my little family, the recipients of all my "ideas." Eight years after the original 7 experiment, we are still practicing tons of what we learned. How wonderful. To Brandon, Gavin, Sydney, Caleb, Ben, and Remy, you are the family of my dreams. Thank you for not moving out when I confiscated all your screens for a month.

Yet again, I'd like to thank the original Council for 7: Jenny, Shonna, Trina, Molly, Becky, and Susana. You helped see through the project in every way, and now it has a new iteration which you deserve credit for. Your support kept the ship afloat. I don't know why any of you ever say yes to me, but I sure love you for it.

I feel so tender toward the team at Abingdon Press for creating a beautiful Christmas version of 7. You have been an utter joy. Thank you for your creativity; you brought real life to this project. I am a delighted new member of your publishing community. You were the perfect home for 7 *Christmas*.

So much sincere love to Austin New Church, the safest, kindest, bravest little faith community I ever did know. I have learned alongside of you what it means to surrender. You've taught me to love my neighbor in wild, shocking ways. I trust you. I am your grateful sister.

ABOUT THE AUTHOR

Jen Hatmaker, sought-after speaker, Big Sister Emeritus, and Chief BFF, is the beloved author of eleven Bible studies and books, including *New York Times* best-sellers *For the Love* and *Of Mess and Moxie*. Jen hosts the award-winning *For the Love* Podcast and leads a tightly knit online community where she reaches millions of people each week, in addition to speaking at events all around the country. Jen and her hubby, Brandon, are founders of Legacy Collective, a giving community that grants millions of dollars around the world. The couple lives on the outskirts of Austin, Texas with their 5 kids—Gavin, Sydney, Caleb, Ben, and Remy—in a 1910-era farmhouse that they overhauled as the stars of the HGTV series *My Big Family Renovation.*

CHRISTMAS 2018

Bethlehem.

The manger.

Mary.

The shepherds.

The star.

The unassuming young almost family from Nazareth.

The angels.

The beautiful baby, Lord at his birth.

I'll never get over that this is the way God did it.

The weary world rejoices still.